Chess
with the
Captain

H.A. Samson

Published in Great Britain by

H. A. Samson,
Manchester House,
BORTH, Dyfed, SY24 5HZ

©1992 H.A. Samson
ISBN 0 9519414 0 2

All rights reserved.
No part of this publication may be reproduced, stored in a retrieval system or transmitted in any form or by any means, electronic, mechanical, photocopying, recording or otherwise without the prior written permission of the author.

Computer set in 12 on 14.9pt Bookman by
ARIOMA Editorial Services,
Gloucester House, High Street,
BORTH, Dyfed. SY24 5HZ

Printed by
Hollen Street Press Ltd.,
141/3 Farnham Road,
SLOUGH,
Berkshire,
SL1 4XB

Cover design by Patrick Smith Associates

CONTENTS

Contents	III
Dedication	IV
Foreword	V
The Ups and Downs of Life	1
Farewell to Perils on the Sea	13
A Spell of Army Life Down Under	21
Back to Sea Again	33
Invitation to the Dance	49

ILLUSTRATIONS

The Author	VI
M.V. *Waimarama*	VII
Adolph Woermann	12
Deck gun on *Waimarama*	20
Sandbags going overboard	20
"Surrey"	32
Building Borth's sea defences	48

The photographs, except the one on P VII, are from the collection of H.A.Samson.

*This book is dedicated to the memory of
Captain John Pearce, Officers and Crew
who perished in
M.V. Waimarama
on the morning of August 13th 1942.*

FOREWORD

The *Waimarama*, commanded by Captain John Pearce, who was Chief Officer when I sailed aboard her, was one of the 14 fast merchant ships that attempted to reach Malta in the *Operation Pedestal* Convoy, in 1942, with a very strong Naval escort that included H.M.S.*Eagle*.

Only 5 ships from this convoy reached Malta and one of those was badly damaged. *Waimarama* was hit by 3 bombs, and she blew up and sank within minutes. In addition to her other cargo, she was carrying T.N.T. and high octane fuel in drums on her deck. From the 104 aboard there were only 21 survivors.

The author in the 1940's

M.V. Waimarama on trials in October 1938
The author was aboard when this picture was taken

Picture via Richard Alexander, Archivist & Historian, Furness Withy Group

The Ups and Downs of Life

I first went to sea in 1937, when I was 17, on the coal burning, refrigerated ship S.S. *Raranga*. She was owned by the Shaw, Savill & Albion Line, and I was paid £3-6-3 per month. I made two voyages in her, then she was laid up, and I was sent to the Harland and Wolff shipyard in Belfast, to join the M.V. *Waimarama*. She was a 535.5 feet long, 13,000 ton refrigerated cargo ship, launched on 31st May, 1938, and capable of carrying a cargo of chilled meat et cetera.

I joined her in 1938, about one year before the outbreak of World War 2. She was a beautiful ship, compared to the old *Raranga*, and on her sea trials, in the Firth of Clyde, she reached $20^1/_2$ knots, which was very fast for a merchant ship in 1938. She was commanded by Captain James Avern R.N.V.R., and I remember feeling very proud of the fact that she flew the Blue Ensign, as opposed to the more usual Red Ensign. On her maiden voyage, from Liverpool to Cape Town, she broke the record, taking just a few hours above fifteen days. On *Raranga*, it had taken twenty-one days

I had joined her as an engineers' steward, at £8-17-6 per month, but on the second voyage, I was made officers' steward, which was a better job, but brought no increase in wages. When we were about half way through the second voyage, going around the Australian coast, out of the blue, I was made captain's steward, through some misconduct by the previous holder of that post. I was quite overwhelmed, and wondered if I would be able to cope with the job, as I knew that the captain entertained a lot of guests, passengers, shipping agents and others.

The ship had accommodation for twelve passengers, and the Chief Steward, Mr. Townrow, gave me a list, and directions on how to mix cocktails, and generally put me at ease. In fact, I got on very well with the captain, whom I always treated with great respect and admiration. My surname being Samson, he decided he would call me Sam. He was a very fit 62 year-old, well-built and 6 feet 2 inches tall. At 6.45 every morning, after his morning tea, he would exercise to the music of gramophone records, which I put on for him. He also had a punch-ball in his bathroom.

While the captain was exercising, I would run his bath. While he was having his bath, I would make his bed and lay out his clothes and uniform for him, and generaly tidy his bedroom. While doing this, occasionally I would hear him banging away at his punch ball. It sounded as though he was quite an expert at it.

While he was dressing, I would lay the table, in his day room, for his breakfast, and bring the breakfast menu from the dining saloon below. After breakfast, I would make his day room spick and span,

Chess with the Captain

sometimes polishing the silver and brass.

One day, when we were homeward bound, from New Zealand via Cape Horn, the sea was calm and I took him his afternoon tea at 3.45, as usual. I found him pondering over a chess problem. As I placed the tray on his table, he looked at me over the top of his glasses and said, "Can you play chess, Sam?"

"Yes, Sir," I said.

"Pull up a chair and let's see how good you are," he said without hesitation.

I was dumbfounded and embarrassed, and wished I had replied "No, Sir".

The captain won, but it was a good game and he concluded by saying, "Not bad. We'll have to play again some time." We were to play many games, in future voyages, and I managed to win a few. This familiarity with the captain never went any further than the chessboard, and even when giving 'Check', I would dutifully say, "Check, Sir."

There was another surprise to come later!

During this passage towards Cape Horn, I can remember the captain and the Chief Officer poring over a chart and, because the weather was so calm, discussing the possibility of sailing through the Straits of Magellan. I have a feeling that this is what we did. We had a part cargo of apples from New Zealand for Rosario, Argentina, quite a long way up the River Plate.

One evening, ashore, at Rosario, I can remember, playing a game of chess, at the rear of a café-cum-pub, (there were also pool tables et cetera there) with a local person, of Spanish appearance, which collected quite a crowd of spectators, probably because I was obviously a foreigner. I won in spectacular fashion, through an *en passant* move. A chess player would know this as an *in passing* move.

We left London Docks on our third voyage, and topped up our general cargo in Hamburg. It was quite frightening to see Nazi troops strutting about, wearing jackboots, carrying rifles, and with their red and black Nazi armbands. Our ship slowly passed by massive German warships as we made our way into the docks. We were only there for the one night before setting sail for Australia via the Cape.

We discharged our general cargo and began loading lamb, butter and wool for the U.K. Our final port of call was Auckland. We were homeward bound by way of the Panama Canal, about five days out from Auckland when war was declared. From then on, the captain took all his meals in his day room, which made things difficult for me, as I hurried up and down two companionways between there and the ship's pantry with different courses.

The ship was now blacked-out at night, and we had a lookout posted in the foremast crow's nest. While we were going through the Panama Canal, the ship was painted battleship grey, from the masthead to the water-line, by a squad of about 100 painters, and in no time the ship was all 'Wet Paint'.

At Colon, we received orders to proceed to Kingston, Jamaica, we thought this was to allow us to join a convoy crossing the Atlantic, but it seemed that

Chess with the Captain

we were too fast for the convoy and we had to proceed alone. The captain instructed the ship's carpenter to construct a dummy gun on the gun platform. (The *Waimarama* was built with a gun platform.) Messages, in code, from the Admiralty were being received frequently. I was very surprised when the captain showed me how to decode them. He explained that it would be very useful, as he would be spending quite a lot of time on the bridge. I can only assume that he thought, because I was intelligent enough to play a fair game of chess, I should be able to manage it.

Most messages were 'Notice to all Shipping', and some gave the known positions of U-boat attacks, wrecks et cetera. When we were in a known danger area, the captain started a zigzag pattern, and it was with some relief, to me, anyway, when a Sunderland flying-boat appeared, and kept an eye on us as we approached the English Channel. We docked safely at London Docks.

I can recall the captain, in conversation with Mr. Pearce, the Chief Officer, saying how determined he was to have a surface gun fitted before the next voyage, and I believe he had quite a tussle with the Admiralty before he was permitted to have a 6" surface gun installed.

After the ship was unloaded, she was moved into dry-dock, and while she was there, in October 1939, a gun was fitted. She must have been one of the first, if not the very first, of the merchant ships to carry a surface gun. She was then moved back out of dry-dock to load a general cargo for Australia. The captain instructed one of the officers to obtain five empty 40-gallon drums. Out of these the ship's carpenter was to make a target for gun practice.

The captain was a widower, and I understood that his wife had been killed in a car accident in Australia. He had a miniature bust of her, head an shoulders, made from ivory and standing about 8 inches high. It was fixed to a shelf to keep it secure when the ship was rolling. When he returned to the ship, the day before she sailed, he brought with him three tubes of ointment, prescribed by a doctor at the St. James's Club in London, where the captain stayed, for the treatment of a nasty-looking phlebitis ulcer which had broken out on the lower part of his left leg. The captain had been staying at the St. James's Club in London while the ship was in the U.K.

The captain had numerous items of silverware, ashtrays, photo frames, et cetera, also a silver cigarette box which held about 100 cigarettes, which I was expected to keep immaculately polished, along with the many brass items. The captain was quite a heavy smoker, and often remarked about the fact. He often used a cigarette-holder, at least, when he was in his day room.

He was also in the habit of drinking about three whiskys and sodas a day, possibly more, if he was entertaining guests. Sometimes, he would ask me how many he had had; although, I never, ever, saw him the worse for drink. He always kept a well-stocked drinks cabinet of spirits and liqueurs.

If I was not in his quarters, I was always at the

end of a bell-push, even, sometimes, just to pour him a scotch and soda!

We were to sail alone, unescorted. The hatches were covered with sandbags, two or three deep. As we were crossing the Bay of Biscay, we ran into a force nine gale, and all the sandbags on the forward hatches were washed over the side, and they took a large section of the ship's rail with them. We had to heave to for a few hours and wait for the wind to abate a little.

We sailed from London with seven passengers aboard, and a doctor working his passage to Australia, and I presume that he would have had to sign on the ship's articles. We also had a stewardess to take care of the passengers' cabins; she was an elderly lady, between 50 and 55 years of age.

Once we were south of the Canaries and in better weather, the captain invited the passengers to have drinks in his quarters. He apologised for not joining them for meals in the dining saloon, and he warned them that within a day or two there would be few rounds of practice fire from our gun. Someone had painted a swastika on the target, which was heaved over the side. The ship was manoeuvred until the target was on our starboard beam, and three rounds were fired from a distance of about two or three miles. The captain seemed quite happy with the result, in spite of the target not being hit.

A few days later, at afternoon tea-time, the captain decided that he would like a game of chess. We had only played about six or seven moves when there was a knock on the door. It was the radio officer with quite a long, coded message. The chess game was abandoned and the message decoded. It was addressed to all ships in Area 9, where, apparently, we happened to be at the time, and the gist of it was, "German ship known to have left Portuguese West African port. Ships in area to keep look-out."

The next morning, the captain carried out his exercises as usual. He took his bath, I bandaged his ulcer, and, at eight o'clock, served him his breakfast. I wondered why, as we had a doctor aboard, the captain got me to see to his leg, and I concluded that he probably doubted whether the man really was a qualified doctor. It was during breakfast that the officer of the watch called in through the bridge door, "Ship off the port bow, sir." The captain got up immediately, picked up his binoculars and went onto the bridge.

He peered at the ship, then said to the chief officer, "We'll take a look at her." We altered course a few points to port. The other ship was heading north, sailing in the opposite direction to us. We passed her close enough to see people aboard waving to us. We waved back. Painted on her side was a large Portuguese flag and the word PORTUGAL in large white letters. A Portuguese flag was flying at her stern, probably run up because of our presence. We had run up the Blue Ensign. Once we had gone past her, the captain said, "That's the bloody Hun."

He had noticed that the port of registration, painted on her stern, had been painted out, even though, according to International law, it should have been there and legible. He sent me below to fetch our radio officer. Although we were committed to keep radio silence, the captain gave him a message, to be transmitted in plain language to the Admiralty. He told the radio officer to let him know as soon as the message had been acknowledged.

We kept on our southerly course, waiting for the acknowledgement to come through. The captain wanted to give the other vessel the impression that we had accepted her as Portuguese, in case she found our radio frequency and jammed our signal. Once the signal was acknowledged, we turned about, and by this time the ship was a mere speck on the horizon. However, with our speed, we quickly caught up with her. We began to circle her, occasionally stopping our engines to allow her to catch up. Our radio officer came to the bridge and reported that she was transmitting messages requesting help, and that she was also answering herself, in a different pitch, as though there was a German vessel or a U-boat in the vicinity. Our gunner suggested to the captain that he carry away her aerial with just one round. This made the captain laugh!

The captain ordered a flag signal to be hoisted, requesting the assistance of a doctor for an operation on a case of appendicitis. The other ship replied to the effect that she did not have a doctor aboard. Meanwhile, we were all wondering which would arrive first, help for her, or the Royal Navy to help us.

Earlier in the voyage, we had received a message that a German surface raider was active in the

Atlantic, and the captain gave the order for our life-boats to be swung out and all hands to keep life-belts handy. During the night, the ship made repeated attempts to ram us, all to no avail. The captain spent all night on the bridge. Next morning, at about 9 o'clock, a speck appeared on the horizon, and it was fingers crossed time!

The captain had already told me that if we were attacked and he was not able to, I was to heave the weighted canvas bag containing the code books over the side.

The ship heading towards us was H.M.S. *Neptune*, which had come at full speed from Cape Verde Islands. As soon as the German ship, which turned out to be the *Adolph Woermann*, recognised her as a British cruiser, she hauled down the Portuguese flag and hoisted a Swastika. She also hoisted a flag signal to say that she was sinking; she had, in fact, been scuttled. Her passengers and crew abandoned ship and their life-boats came alongside *Waimarama*. Although the *Neptune* sent a boarding party to try and save her, they were too late. *Neptune* then pulled away from her, and shelled her to hasten the sinking.

Our captain called down to the German captain, "Kapitän, I asked you for a doctor yesterday, and you said you did not have one. Who is that?" He pointed at a man wearing a uniform which he recognised as being that of a German doctor. The German captain just spread his arms in despair, as if to say, "What could I do?"

H.M.S. *Neptune* took the survivors aboard, then their crew lined the rails and gave us three cheers. They were flying a flag signal reading, "God Speed to Cape Town". Needless to say, our captain was the toast of every port of call round the coasts of Australia and New Zealand, and so it was a very busy time for me, serving drinks and refreshments to guests. A photograph appeared on the front page of the local newspapers at every port. It was taken by one of our women passengers, and by looking closely, one could just see a German life-boat heading towards us, also our own life-boat davits swung out.

The captain was later awarded an O.B.E., which he proudly showed me during a later voyage.

It may be as well to mention here that, three weeks after this encounter, the Nazi pocket battleship *Graf Spee* was sighted and engaged by H.M.S. *Exeter, Ajax* and *Achilles*, and was forced to run for Montevideo, where she was later scuttled. It is, therefore, possible that she might have been in the South Atlantic at that time.

The Ups and Downs of Life

HMS Neptune (left) and Adolph Woermann (right) photographed November 25th, 1939 by H.A. Samson

Editor's Note:
The *Adolph Woermann* (8,577 tons) sailed from Lobito, in Portuguese West Africa, on 18th November, 1939, in company with a larger vessel, the *Windhuk* (16,662 tons). The *Adolph Woermann* was scuttled approximately one week later, during the encounter mentioned above, and 162 passengers and crew were picked up.
The photograph above was taken by the author and the film developed and printed in his cabin.

Farewell to Perils on the Sea.

At the start of another voyage, we left Liverpool to rendezvous with two other fast ships, and to sail together with them through the North Channel and into the Atlantic. I was told that these two ships were the *Arandora Star* and a troopship. Both were torpedoed during the night, with very heavy loss of life. We must have been under orders not to stop, for we zigzagged our way out of trouble, although a look-out reported a torpedo track heading in our direction, but it was not confirmed, and if it had been there, it missed us. Later, we learned that the troopship had been taking a large party of army, navy and air force personnel to Canada for training, and many perished that night. The *Arandora Star* had 1,500 internees aboard, on their way to an internment camp in Canada. 470 Italians and 143 Germans lost their lives when the ship went down.

Now alone, we headed out into the Atlantic, going much further out than we would normally have done, before heading south for Cape Town. When the officer of the watch called to the captain, "Ship dead ahead, sir," the captain immediately ordered the helmsman to go hard a port, and steer 185. He then ordered a signal to be sent by Aldis lamp, "What ship?" Back came the reply, "What ship?" By now there were three officers on the bridge, and they all agreed that it appeared as if the ship had altered course and was now heading in our direction.

The captain sent me below to fetch Mr. Margitson, the chief engineer, and to inform him of the situation with some urgency. The captain asked the Chief how much more speed he could let him have. I cannot recall his reply, but we seemed to be getting a move on, and the ship vibrated more than usual. We altered course during the night, and there was no sign of the ship in the morning, so we never did discover just what ship it was. I think I must have made six or seven voyages in the *Waimarama*, but the last voyage I made aboard her was when we carried a load of ammunition, bombs of all descriptions, shells et cetera, and were headed for Piraeus, Greece.

While I was a member of the crew of *Waimarama*, she was never in convoy; it's just possible that the only time she was in convoy was probably for "Operation Pedestal".

The Mediterranean was closed to shipping, and so we had to go round the Cape and through the Suez Canal. The ship had been fitted with paravanes, which, as I recall, were only used once. I got the impression that the captain thought that they slowed the ship down too much, bearing in mind that we were usually sailing in swept channels. The ship also had degaussing cables wound round the hull to neutralize magnetic mines.

We were sailing north, at night, off the East African coast, when we had a very near collision with

Chess with the Captain

an Arab Dhow. Both the dhow and we were, of course, blacked-out and the Arab dhow was a fair sized vessel. We missed her by a matter of yards, and we could hear Arab voices shouting excitedly as we passed by. Our captain was very angry that the ship had not been showing navigation lights, being that it was probably a neutral vessel.

We arrived in Aden, dropped anchor and awaited orders, as it was known that the Germans had invaded Greece and were advancing rapidly towards Piraeus, our original destination. We waited in Aden for three or four days before receiving orders to proceed to Alexandria, and then we set off up the Red Sea to Suez. On our arrival there we found the White Star liner *Georgic* burning fiercely from stem to stern. She had obviously been attacked, probably bombed, very recently. We continued through the Canal, to the wail of air raid sirens, and eventually reached Port Said. We were to make the journey to Alexandria at night, because of the risk of attack by enemy aircraft, who were poised to attack and occupy Crete.

We set sail at dusk, hugging the coast as closely as we dared. The captain intended to spend the night on the bridge, but instead decided to lie fully clothed on his settee, after leaving instructions with the second officer to call him if the echo sounder graph showed less than five fathoms.

Next morning we were aground on a sandbank. When I took the captain's tea up to him, he was having a heated argument with the second officer. Apparently, the echo sounder graph had indicated that the captain should have been called about an hour before the ship ran aground. The captain lost his temper and struck the second officer, who drew my attention to the assault. I had been steward to the second officer, for about six weeks, while I was the officers' steward, before I became captain's steward, and I found him not very easy to get on with. He even used to complain about the volume of the captain's record player, during his exercising, and would ask me to turn the volume down. However, there we were, stuck like a sitting duck, with a cargo of explosives aboard, and far too close to enemy action for comfort. A tug and a small coaster came from Alexandria to try and tow us off. We were aground for somewhere between six and eight hours. After the tow lines had parted twice, she slid off the sandbank at the third attempt, but our steering gear was damaged, and it was with some difficulty, and help from the tug, that we limped into Alexandria.

I think we were very lucky not to have been spotted by enemy aircraft, while we were aground.

The ship was unloaded, but owing to the damaged steering gear we were unable to sail. It took three weeks for a new part to be cast, machined and fitted. In the meantime, the aircraft carrier H.M.S. *Formidable*, with a gaping hole in her port bow, entered the harbour. A barge was moored alongside her, where it was nearly half filled with the bodies of her casualties. The barge was then towed away and moored just in front of the *Waimarama* - not a pretty sight! Eventually, the bodies were taken away for burial.

Chess with the Captain

The captain and chief engineer would often go to the engineering workshop where the part for the steering gear was being made, and from their conversation, I deduced that Alexandria was just about the worst place to be when in need of such a part.

One morning, I think it was a Wednesday, the captain sprang another surprise. He asked me if I would like to go to a race meeting that afternoon. "Yes, please, Sir," I said. Apparently some of his friends had invited him. I found it hard to believe that a race meeting was actually taking place while Field Marshal Rommel and his troops were threatening Egypt from the Western Desert!

The captain's friends sent a chauffeur driven car to pick us up and take us to the race meeting, which was packed with officers and other ranks from all three branches of the services, and, of course, Egyptians. I soon discovered why I had been invited to go along. I was the one who had to join the long queue at the tote window, to place the bets and collect any returns, but I enjoyed it and found it made a change from the depressing and monotonous stay in the harbour. After the racing, the captain stayed ashore, to dine with his friends, and he sent me back to the ship by taxi. The same thing happened again the following week.

During our stay in Alexandria, there were enemy air raids nearly every night, and a few by day. Nearly all were high altitude attacks, out of range of the anti-aircraft fire. Moored not far from us was a British mine-laying submarine. Every four or five days it was loaded with supplies for our forces in Tobruk, which held out against Rommel's army for a very long time. The submarine crept along at night, hugging the coast, submerging when necessary, I suppose!

When we had an occasional evening ashore, my mates and I would go along to the Fleet Club in Alexandria to enjoy a few drinks and a game of Tombola, or Bingo as they call it today. The Fleet Club was always packed with servicemen. We usually found ourselves walking back to the ship during an air raid. Then, at last, the part we needed in order to repair the steering gear was ready and on its way to the ship; the engineers fitted it, tested it and found it satisfactory, and the ship was ready for sea. We received orders to sail, in ballast, to Australia.

Hugging the coast-line, we made our way back to Port Said at night, and the captain stayed on the bridge. We went through the Canal to Suez, and down the Red Sea to cross the Indian Ocean to Fremantle. It was while we were crossing the Indian Ocean that I played what was to be my last game of chess with the captain. With all the games of chess that I played with the captain, I always felt ill at ease and embarrassed, especially when one of his officers came to his quarters, for some reason.

We arrived at Fremantle to refuel and take on water, then we sailed for Melbourne. It was while we were on our way to Melbourne that the captain told me that he would be leaving the ship when we arrived there, but he did not tell me why, although I surmised that it might be as a result of his fracas with Mr. Grant, the second officer.

Chess with the Captain

At Melbourne, I carried the captain's bags down the gangway to the car that had come to collect him. He shook hands with me, thanked me for my services, and I never saw, or heard of him again.

Mr. Pearce, the chief officer, was now acting captain, and he was a very nice person. I had looked after his cabin, too, while I was an officers' steward. He did not move into the captain's quarters, at least during the trip to Sydney, but he might have done so later. The reason I do not know whether he moved in afterwards is because I jumped ship at Sydney. I watched the *Waimarama* sail out of Sydney Harbour, having done what I did because I thought I might be called as a witness, in a maritime court, to the assault made by the captain on the second officer.

A few days later I joined the Australian Army.

Deck gun on Waimarama.

The author is on the right.

Sandbags going overboard in the Bay of Biscay.

See Page 7

A Spell of Army Life Down Under

I first met John Dunn at the recruiting office in Sydney, New South Wales, where we became friends and agreed to join the Artillery Signals. I signed on first, and I think my Army Number was something like NX94298, which would have made John's number NX94299. We were both transported by army truck, along with other recruits, to an army training camp at Cowra, N.S.W., which lay about 100 miles west of Sydney. I had joined up under my real name, Harold Austin Samson, and given my correct London address.

We had the usual army square-bashing, training day after day, then doing it all again, with rifles. Because we were in Signals, we were trained to use field radios, vocal and Morse code, and signal by light and heliograph. They taught us to lay telephone wires from the back of a truck travelling at 30 m.p.h., and to pick them back up again, but not at 30 m.p.h. this time. At the Cowra camp we lived in huts, with about twenty men to each. Later, during the war, this Cowra camp was used to hold Japanese prisoners of war, and when it was subsequently used for a film called "The Cowra Break-out", I hoped I might have been able to recognize some land-marks, but I was out of luck.

The main purpose of the Artillery Signals was, of

course, to establish lines of communication between outposts and the command post and gun positions using whatever means were easiest, or possible. Using a heliograph was quite tricky; it consisted of a Simplex mirror for signalling against the sun, and a Duplex when working with the sun behind you! Contact having been established, adjustments had to be made continuously, as the sun moved across the sky. With this in mind, some of us, of which I was one, were divided into five groups, representing a command post and four outposts, and sent off on a five day training exercise. Our orders were to make contact with the command post and with each other using radio and light at night and heliograph during the day. Each group had rations for five days, and we each knew the map reference of the command post, but not that of the other groups. It was, of course, a map-reading exercise as well as communication! We had first to make contact with the command post, who would then give us the map references of the other groups, so that eventually, and with luck, we should all be able to contact any group.

Although we had been given rations, there were no tents, and we slept in the open. The field radio, known as a 101, as I seem to recall, had worked well in training, when used over just 200 to 300 yards, but it was useless when used over a few miles, and our best contacts were made with lights, heliograph and using Morse code.

On our return to camp we were given a week's leave, and as I had no home in Australia, so John Dunn invited me to come and stay at his home, which

Chess with the Captain

was on the outskirts of Sydney, about a twenty minute train ride from the city, although I have forgotten the name of his district. When we returned to camp, we had orders that the whole unit was being sent to Brisbane, where the 1st Medium Artillery Regiment was being formed.

All signals personnel were encouraged to learn how to handle a motorcycle; there were machines available for us to practise on, and we could use them whenever we had any spare time. After just a few runs round the track, John and I both obtained Dispatch Rider's Licences. By this time, however, I was very homesick and worried about the folks at home, what with the Blitz, the bombing and everything. I was also worried that the cash allotment to my mother would have been stopped. I had also realised that there was no likelihood that I would be required for any maritime court martial, if there ever were to be one, because Captain Avern, being an officer and a gentleman, would in any case have admitted the misdemeanour.

A sergeant, three truck drivers and I, with a motorcycle, were ordered to load our vehicles onto goods wagons. The trucks were loaded up with tents and other equipment to travel to Brisbane. Our four railway wagons were hitched onto the back of eight or nine others, and we were advised that we should be sleeping in the back of the army trucks.

We had rations for about a week, as well as all our own kit, and rifles and ammunition, provided, presumably, so that we could defend our equipment. After a few hours travelling, the train often pulled onto a siding and sat there, sometimes for hours, in the middle of nowhere, the countryside around us like barren desert. To pass the time, we played cards in the back of one of the trucks, or used our .303 rifles for target practice.

There might be a few isolated homesteads near some of the sidings, standing in little patches of green grass. The long wait in the sidings for us was, of course, to allow other trains to pass through. When we eventually arrived at the Queensland border, we had to off-load our trucks and reload them onto different railway wagons, because the railway gauge was different here from what it was in N.S.W. We set off again soon afterwards, and had been rolling along for about five hours when, suddenly, there was smoke rising from one of our trucks. The engine driver had spotted it from his cab, and he stopped the train and sent his fireman back to warn us that one of our vehicles was on fire. We pulled out the burning tents and extinguished the fire, but we must have lost eight or nine of our tents. The fire was attributed to a spark from the engine, but, in fact, we all knew it was more probably caused by a cigarette end dropped by one of us while we were playing cards in the truck a short time before.

When we arrived at the Brisbane camp, our unit was already there, having arrived from Cowra a few days earlier. The camp was under canvas on what was a temporary site. Once all personnel had been assembled, we were to move to a new site some eight to ten miles out of Brisbane. A convoy of half a dozen trucks was sent to Toowooba, to collect stores, more

Chess with the Captain

tents et cetera, but they had left camp without the necessary paperwork. A dispatch rider was called for.

"Anyone here got a dispatch rider's licence?" asked one of the officers. Up went my hand, and I was sent to catch up the convoy and hand over the papers. Until now I had never ridden on a public road, except for the short journey from the railhead. I put the papers in the pocket of my greatcoat, tied the coat to the pillion, and off I went. I had been given the route to Toowooba that the convoy was to take, and everything was going along quite well until I noticed a strong smell of petrol, and saw that fuel was squirting out of two small holes at the top of the carburettor. I did not know the first thing about a petrol engine, but I thought my situation was quite dangerous, with petrol squirting onto a hot engine. I decided to fill up the carburettor, then switch the petrol off, and run as far as it would take me. The bike would run for two or three miles on a carburettor full of petrol, and that is how I eventually arrived at Toowooba, to find that the convoy had arrived several hours earlier. During one of the stops, I suddenly realised that my greatcoat was missing, and guessed that it must have fallen off because of the bumpy roads I had been riding on. I pictured myself in the guardroom, and in a great deal of bother, on a charge of losing the dispatches but, on the contrary, I was congratulated on getting there, and nobody seemed to worry much about the fact that I had lost the papers. And, of course, the only thing wrong with the bike was that the float chamber in the carburettor was stuck down. The bike was put right, and I escorted the convoy back to Brisbane the next day.

The Australians like to gamble, and John and I would sometimes visit a 'Two-Up' game, which was always being played somewhere out of sight of the camp. The punters would form a circle, and the Boxer (umpire) would invite anyone to spin 'heads'. The person doing this would usually be the one to stake the most. The spin only takes place when the stake is covered, either by one player, or several others making smaller bets. Anyone putting up a £10 stake and then spinning heads four times would make £160. The spinner can drop out with his winnings at any time during the game, usually after tipping the 'Boxer'. The game was played with two English penny coins, and a sudden death game played with three.

The spinner placed the coins, tails up, on a piece of wood, that had some special name which I have since forgotten, and up they would go. If the 'Boxer' was unhappy about a spin he would call "Void" before the coins hit the ground. The game was, of course, illegal, and lookouts were posted at various points, to warn of the approach of officers or red-caps. Hundreds of pounds changed hands at these games. An English pound was worth £1-5-0 Australian at that time.

Obviously, with only two coins, one head and one tail, the spin would have to be made again. To win it had to be the two coins heads, or tails. It was quite exciting just to watch a game in progress, to hear voices calling, "Any money, heads," or, "Any money tails." It was quite amazing to see wads of notes changing hands at the spin of two coins.

The regiment moved to the new site, which was a wooded area with quite a bit of grass about, for a change. We were to train with 6-inch Howitzer artillery pieces, and eventually went to a firing range for practice. We slept under canvas outside Brisbane, and after Reveille we had to walk about a mile to a river, where we washed and shaved to the cries of the kookaburra. We were advised to carry a snake-bite outfit consisting of a razor blade and a length of string, and we were instructed what to do with it. Not all the snakes we encountered were dangerous, however. On one occasion, John and I were on some kind of training exercise, on the outskirts of the camp, when we came across a homestead, built up on timbers that held it clear of the ground. The people invited us in for tea, and I nudged John when I spotted quite a big snake curled up in a corner. Apparently it was a pet, kept, as we would keep a cat, to dispose of mice and other vermin. They said it was a carpet snake, and quite harmless. I think that John, who was an Australian, was just as surprised as me to see it there.

I went to Brisbane on a pass, by army truck to the station and then by train, and had a look at the riverside, to see what ships were in. At a wharf, which I knew as Borthwicks, where I had docked many times on *Waimarama*, I saw what I recognised as a Blue Funnel ship. I thought she would be sailing for the U.K. She was loading wool bales, and as I knew these were usually the last items of cargo to be loaded, I guessed she must be nearly ready to sail. Stow away, I thought. By tomorrow or the day after I could be on my way home.

I walked up and down the riverside, thinking it over and trying to work out how I could get aboard. The old Brisbane trams went clunking up and down the road, while I sat in a small shelter used by passengers waiting for a cable ferry. When it got dark, I walked back to the wharf. The dockers were still loading the wool bales, so I waited for them to finish, as it was already quite late and I expected them to stop work at any time. Eventually, they did stop, and I got over the boundary wall and hid amongst the wool bales on the quay. These bales were about 4 feet 6 inches square. I could now see the ship's gangway, but there was a watchman at the top. I thought, sooner or later he is going to wander along to the ship's galley to make himself a cup of tea. Then, suddenly, all the dockers streamed out again and carried on loading. Worse, they were gradually working their way towards the place where I was hiding.

I looked round for a spot to move to, if I got the chance. I edged back to the bales that were furthest away, and eventually managed to get behind a hut. I need not have worried, for not long afterwards the dockers stopped work again, this time for good; I saw them going out through the dock gates. As I thought, the watchman on the gangway suddenly strolled along the deck, towards the direction of the ship's galley. I walked up the gangway and got into one of the lifeboats. About an hour after this, I decided it might be a good idea to take a look at the crew list, which on Shaw Savill & Albion ships was usually on display in the saloon area. So I went to take a look, but, to my dismay it was all in Chinese. It seemed as if, from the captain downwards, the whole crew were Chinese. Then the penny dropped. The Blue Funnel Line had some ships that traded only in the Far East, and this was one of them. She was probably not going to the U.K. at all.

It was clear that I had to get off her, and I walked to the gangway, past the watchman, said good night, and walked out through the dock gates, and nobody so much as challenged me. In any case, I knew that I was already AWOL, and I had no choice other than to return to camp. Although I passed red-caps at the station, I was not challenged. From the station, I started to walk the five miles into camp, but after I had gone part of the way an army lorry pulled up, picked me up and took me back to camp. After I had had a wash and shave to smarten myself up, I was brought before the C.O. He asked me why I had gone AWOL. I told him the truth, and said exactly what I had done, then I asked him if I could have a transfer to the British Army. "No chance," he said. He then gave me a lecture, ending up with the warning that in war-time deserters are shot. He sentenced me to three weeks in the field kitchen peeling potatoes, and loss of pay.

Later, the regiment spent a week, or so, at the firing range, and I was back mainly on dispatch riding duties. After we had been back in camp for about ten days, an officer came to the camp, to ask for volunteers from any of us who had any experience of docks, cranes, shipping et cetera to join a new 'Dock Operating Unit', which was being formed at Townsville. Up went my hand, and my name and number were taken and, within seven days, I found myself heading for Townsville. Although I did not really have any practical experience of loading and unloading ships, I had seen it done very often.

The unit was based just about twenty minutes walk away from the town, and I had, of course, been here many times before on *Waimarama* and *Raranga*. We were to be trained to drive cranes, and in dock work in general, to operate the docks at Port Moresby, New Guinea. Some of the unit were already at the docks and under instruction. The ship they were working on was called the *Fort Pine*. I found out, while having a drink in a pub not far from the harbour, that this ship was short of three Able Bodied Seamen (A/Bs). Now, I had never been an A/B, but, there again, I more or less knew what the duties were, and I thought I could manage them. The biggest problem was that I would have to capable of taking the wheel. This was something else I had very often seen done, for I was on the bridge quite a lot on the *Waimarama*, serving coffee et cetera to the captain and pilots, or cleaning brass portholes, quite close to the helmsman, and I had often thought I would sooner have his job than mine.

I knew, too, that the helmsman always repeated any order he was given, and whereas I would answer the captain, or any officer, with "Yes, sir", the seamen nearly always answered, "Aye aye, sir". I immediately made up my mind. I had not been at the camp long enough to be known very well, so it was now or never! I bought a pair of civvy trousers, two shirts, shoes and a woolly hat like most sailors wear. Next, I walked into a public toilet as an ordinary sapper, shoved my army gear into a bag, screwed my Aussie army hat into the space behind the toilet cistern, and emerged as a civilian. I dumped my army uniform somewhere near the beach, then made my way to the shipping office, where I told them that I had heard that there was a ship in the harbour with vacancies for Able Seamen. The man in the office said, "Yes, there is. The Captain is coming here tomorrow morning, at ten o'clock, to sign someone on."

I booked into a house for bed and breakfast, and the woman there asked me a lot of questions. I said I had come to join a ship in the harbour. I had begun to feel a bit apprehensive by now, and wondered whether I would get away with it. I decided to change my name to Cyril Thompson, and I altered my writing style for my new signature. The shipping office was only ten minutes walk away from my lodgings, and I arrived there before ten o'clock. The captain turned up, and he wanted to know how I came to be in Australia, as he had noted my London address. I told him I had missed a ship in Sydney. He did not pursue his enquiry, and he must have been relieved to have found at least two of the three crew members he needed. The other chap he signed on was a Welshman from Cardiff, known to me as Taffy, and whose surname I have forgotten.

The captain took us both back to the ship, and as I walked up the gangway, I kept a very low profile, knowing that the unit I was deserting was actually loading the ship with sugar. It appeared that we were due to sail on the following day. Every time I saw one of the army officers strutting about the ship, I kept thinking that any minute now I was going to be recognized by somebody, so I kept out of the way as much as possible. When my new shipmates noticed my lack of gear, I said I had left it all on the ship I had missed, and they came up with various bits of clothing for me, for which I was very grateful. They were a good crowd.

'Surrey', the sailor's home by the sea, to which he came after his sailing days were done.

Back to Sea Again

At last, the ship's beams were put in, and we Able Seamen replaced the hatch boards and canvas covers and battened down; lowered and clamped down the ship's derricks, and although the ship was not fully loaded, it appeared that we were to top up at Melbourne. I was pleased to see the army unit leave the ship and drive away in their trucks. We were to sail on the tide the following morning.

My next problem was the wheel, and I was hoping that I would not be the one to have to take the ship out of harbour. The pilot came aboard next morning. I happened to be doing some job on the boat-deck, just below the starboard side of the bridge when the second officer walked out from the wheelhouse and said, "Ere, Thompson, take the wheel!" I don't know if it was by design, or just Sod's Law, but there it was: my worst fear was being realised. "Aye aye, sir," I said.

The ship was facing inland, so it would have to turn about, in order to go through the harbour entrance. A tug was standing by to assist in the manoeuvre. "Let go for'ard," shouted the pilot, and gave the signal to the stern to tighten the back-spring. The ship began to move slowly forward, the tug taking the strain and pulling her round. "Let go aft," the pilot shouted. "Half ahead. Hard a starboard."

"Hard a starboard," I answered, and spun the wheel hard over. By now the ship was nearly round. The pilot signalled to let go the tug. "Midships," he called. "Midships," I answered. "Check her," called the pilot. The ship now had steerage-way, and I knew I had to put the helm to port to check her, but I did not know how much.

"She's still swinging," called the pilot. I gave it more to port and she stopped swinging. I let the wheel spin back to midships and the ship moved nicely through the harbour entrance. Once clear, the pilot called, "Stop engines," said his goodbyes to the captain, and, as the ship moved slowly ahead, the pilot clambered over the side and into his launch. All the time I had been standing at the wheel of *Fort Pine*, one thought went through my head: I knew my life was at stake, and depended upon the success of my performance. I had not forgotten the warning about deserters in wartime being shot.

"Full ahead," called the captain; the ship's telegraph rang as the lever was pushed to 'Full Ahead'. "Steer 143," called the captain. "143, sir," I answered. I found it quite surprisingly easy to handle the wheel. In about ten minutes, another A/B came to relieve me, and he told me that I had been allocated the 12-4 watch.

I felt quite pleased with myself, that I had coped so far, but I was still a bit worried about the stop at Melbourne, and I would much have preferred to have been leaving Australia without any further ports of call. On the 12-4 watch there were three A/Bs. One did two hours at the wheel and one hour on stand-by, which entailed sitting in the mess-room and making tea, and then one hour on lookout duty. On the next watch, when it would be daytime, we did one hour lookout and one hour working, under instructions from the bosun, and then two hours on the wheel. The third one of the watch would do one hour lookout, two hours working and then another hour on lookout. The pattern altered on every watch.

The 12-4 watch was always considered to be the worst, but it did not bother me. I found steering the ship at night, on a calm sea, was quite easy. The compass was illuminated and magnified, and I had often stood at the wheel of the *Waimarama*, lost in make-believe, while she was in port or at anchor. In fact, under calm conditions, it would have been quite easy to fall asleep. In rough conditions, or even in moderate conditions, wind and heavy seas kept the helmsman quite active and occupied to keep the ship on course! The ship, of course, was blacked-out, and we were sailing through the Great Barrier Reef, as I had done many times before, but this time I was an Able Seaman, and had a much easier job then being a captain's steward.

We arrived at Melbourne, where I was horrified to see two army officers come aboard. I thought, this is it! They were talking to the captain, and I walked by with the rest of the crew, and removed canvas covers from the hatches and hatch boards ready for loading to begin. All the while, I was waiting for a hand to land on my shoulder and someone to ask me if I was the seaman who had signed on in Townsville. But, no, after about twenty minutes they left the ship, and I never discovered what they had been talking to the captain about.

It looked as though we were going to be in port for two or three days, and the crew was advised that it could have a sub on its wages. I went ashore with Taffy and bought myself a suit, shirts and all the other things I needed. It seemed strange to be called Cyril, but I was slowly getting used to my new name. Taffy and I went and had a few drinks. I was not a big drinker, and I really did not like beer. I often used to wonder how anyone could become an alcoholic, and I would describe myself, if anything, as more of a social drinker.

One of the A/Bs aboard was a very good pianist, and we had all heard him play. If we were in a pub where there was a piano, he would sit down and give us a tune. Somebody in Melbourne gave him a piano, old but in working order, apart from a couple of missing keys. With captain's permission, it was hoisted aboard and put in our mess-room. I wonder if that sailor is alive today, or any others, who remember a piano in the mess room of the *Fort Pine*, and if he remembers the sing-songs we had on *Fort Pine*. I forget his name, but recall that he lived in East London, spoke with a Cockney accent and was about my own age.

We battened down the hatches, lowered the derricks and set sail for Fremantle, where we were to refuel and take on fresh water. She was an oil-fired

Chess with the Captain

steam ship, and now that I had got the hang of it, I was not asked again to take the ship out of harbour. We carried on where we had left off with our watches. The Captain signed on another A/B while we were at Fremantle, and now our ship's crew was complete.

We left Fremantle, bound for Bombay with a cargo of sugar. When we were 24 hours out from Fremantle, it was realised that the new A/B we had signed on was missing. The ship was searched, but we found no sign of him, and it was known that he was on board after the ship had sailed. The captain turned about and we retraced our course for some four hours, but saw no sign of the missing man, so he was presumed lost overboard, and we got back on course for Bombay. Apart from this incident, it was an uneventful trip, except for a very large whale that swam alongside our port quarter. It seemed to be actually rubbing itself against the side of the ship. This was at night, and the noise the whale made when it breathed could be heard at the wheel, which is where I was when I heard it first. I saw the creature when I was relieved and on my way back to the mess-room.

There was not anybody aboard who played chess; perhaps the captain did. The smell of our cargo of sugar was terrible, a sickly aroma, made worse by the calm conditions. We arrived at Bombay. While the ship was being unloaded, we painted the ship's funnel, from bosun's chairs, and started painting the hull.

When the unloading was completed, we set sail for Karachi, to load linseed for the U.K. We completed the hull painting, during loading.

The Mediterranean was still closed to shipping, and we had to sail right round the Cape, but first we refuelled at Durban, then rounded the Cape, bound for Freetown, Sierra Leone, where we were to assemble for a convoy sailing to the U.K. We dropped anchor in the bay, where a number of other ships were already at anchor and waiting.

All the ships' captains were summoned to meet aboard the ship of the convoy's commodore, and a launch was sent round to pick them up. I presumed the discussion was about the allocation of positions in the convoy, what action to take in the event of an emergency, zigzag patterns et cetera. If the escort ships flew a black flag, it meant that enemy aircraft were approaching, and a black pennant was a U-boat warning.

Eventually, we weighed anchor, and I was ordered below, to the chain locker, to stow the anchor chain. It was supposed to be a self-stowing locker, but it evidently needed a bit of coaxing now and then. So far, this had been my worst job, as mud from the sea bed made it stink to high heaven. We took up our position, third ship in the third column from the starboard side. We no longer had to follow a compass course, we just tailed the ship ahead, which was difficult at night, for the ship ahead showed just a small bluish light. Now and then, the officer of the watch would have to telephone the engine room and ask for an increase in speed by a few revolutions, or for a slight decrease, when we wanted to catch up with the ship ahead, or we were closing to fast. As we passed Gibraltar, more ships joined the convoy, some were

Chess with the Captain

Liberty ships from America.

Suddenly, during the night, we heard depth charges, or was it a ship being torpedoed? Yes, it was depth charges. We were on the outskirts of the Bay of Biscay, and we could see the escort flying a black flag. Soon afterwards, a large German aircraft, probably a Focke-Wulf Condor, appeared and circled the convoy, keeping well out of range of the escort's A.A. fire, and the ships that had guns. *Fort Pine* did not have guns at the time. We knew then that the enemy knew the convoy's position, but in spite of this, and many black flags and pennants, not one ship was lost.

I had other worries. I wondered what to do when we arrived back in Britain, as I had no papers, nothing to prove my identity and I was under an assumed name. We were about to sail up the Manchester Ship Canal, and when we got there, I considered jumping overboard, but the water looked filthy. In the end, I decided to write a letter telling the truth, and explaining that I was not really an Able Seaman either. I gave it to the captain's steward to pass on to him. The captain sent for me, and in the presence of immigration officers, he said he found it hard to believe that I had not been an A/B before, and that I was one of the best A/Bs aboard the ship. I had then to wait until two police detectives came and collected me and took me to a police station in Manchester.

Looking back, I wish I had asked the captain of the *Fort Pine* if the two army officers who came aboard at Melbourne had been looking for a Sapper Samson NX94298, being that his ship had just arrived from

Townsville. I shall never know the answer now. My shipmates were also very surprised to see me being taken away by the two detectives.

On the way, my escorts stopped at a pub and I bought a round of drinks. They knew I had been at sea for nearly two months, and they thought I deserved one. I remember that one of the detectives was Detective Sergeant Winterbottom. How can you forget a name like that? They were both very nice to me, and they explained that they had to contact the Shaw, Savill & Albion Company and Australia House, in London, to find out if anyone was going to take any action against me. I had visions of being sent back to Australia and shot.

I spent all night in the police station, not locked up, just sitting around and drinking tea. At last, the message came that neither would take any action, providing I carried on working in the Merchant Service. I breathed a deep sigh of relief. I was free to go home and to revert to my real name, Harold Austin Samson. I had been away for nearly two years, and my mother and sisters could not believe it when I appeared at the door of my home.

After a week at home, I reported as an A/B to the shipping office and was sent to join a ship called *Tordene* at Liverpool. We were to sail with a general cargo to Halifax, Nova Scotia. We left in convoy, passing through the North Channel, and crossed the North Atlantic with just two escorting frigates. A few depth charges were dropped, but we arrived safely at Halifax, where we loaded a cargo of timber, stacked

Chess with the Captain

high, as deck cargo, then we headed for home. During the return journey we hit bad weather, and during the storm our cargo shifted and we developed quite a bad list. We lost a lot of speed and were unable to keep up with the convoy, but an escorting frigate would come back now and again, keeping an eye on us. I think the captain considered jettisoning some of the cargo in order to trim her up a bit, but we did not do this, and so we limped back into Liverpool, shadowed by a Sunderland flying boat.

When I next reported to the shipping office, I was asked if I would be prepared to go on a gunnery course at the D.E.M.S. Training Centre, H.M.S. *Chrysanthemum*, at Leigh-on-Sea, Essex. I agreed, and was trained to use different types of A.A. machine guns and the Oerlikon cannon. When I had completed the course, I was sent to join the *Fort Fitzgerald* at Avonmouth. She was loading a mixed cargo of ammunition and N.A.A.F.I. supplies, also a deck cargo of army lorries and jeeps, and we did not find out where we were heading until after we had put out to sea and joined the convoy. *Fort Fitzgerald* had an anti-aircraft gun, a 4.7, I think it was, and two Oerlikons, one on each side of the bridge, which was to be my action station. There were others aboard who had gunnery certificates, but in the event of any action, the one standing nearest the gun would take over.

We were heading for Italy, and formed part of a very large convoy with an aircraft carrier at its centre. This was a merchant ship which had been converted into a carrier. When we were approaching the Bay of

Biscay, sure enough, the German Focke Wulf appeared and circled the convoy. As soon as the escorts hoisted the black flag, we were called to "action stations". I was on the Oerlikon, the starboard side of the bridge, but this time it was not long before high level bombers arrived and dropped a number of bombs at random. One ship, on our starboard beam, had a very near miss. Other bombs fell harmlessly amongst the convoy. I had thought that, perhaps, a fighter plane would have taken off from the carrier, but to do this it would have had to manoeuvre into position against the wind, which would have been difficult in the centre of a convoy.

Two or three ships opened up, but the aircraft were well out of range. I was at my gun and fired a few rounds. At least I established that it worked alright. Every third round was a tracer. Once again, quite a number of depth charges were dropped on the convoy, but none of the ships were lost. At Gibraltar, a big batch of American Liberty ships joined us and we proceeded through the Mediterranean towards Italy. At last, I found a crew member who played chess: the bosun. We played quite a few times, and as we were of about equal strength, they were very good games.

The Allies had air supremacy in the Mediterranean at this time, since the Nazis had been defeated in the Western Desert, but attacks on the convoys in this area were still possible. In fact, the attack on us came from a rather different direction than we anticipated. A really bad electrical storm, the worst I ever experienced to this day, hit us. I was on lookout when it was at its height, and there was no way I could take cover. I could hear the lightning striking; it seemed to be right beside me continuously, and I could not understand why I was not struck, but on reflection, I imagine that a ship must be about the best sort of lightning conductor possible, its steel hull connecting straight to the sea and to earth. Whoever heard of anyone being struck by lightning on a ship? By the time the storm had eased off a bit, I was relieved from lookout and went to make a cup of tea. We arrived at our destination, a small port called Torre Annunziata situated at the base of Mount Vesuvius, and while we were there, Ossie, a shipmate, and I visited the ruins of Pompeii.

The unloading was done by Royal Engineers, I think, and when it was completed the ship dropped anchor in the bay and awaited orders. Once there were twelve or fourteen empty ships assembled, we proceeded in convoy to Cape Bone, off Tunisia, not far from the spot where *Waimarama* was bombed and sunk. Soon after we had left Torre Annunziata, a ship waiting, at anchor, to be unloaded, was bombed and blew up. This must have been about a week or two after the Allied landing at Anzio, 60 to 70 miles north of Naples.

At Cape Bone, all the empty ships in the convoy took aboard thousands of German prisoners of war, from the Western Desert Campaign, to take them along the coast to Algiers. They were placed in the holds of the ships with very few British soldiers, armed with Tommy guns, to guard them. It was really quite a distressing situation. The commodore of the convoy instructed all ships, at a given signal, to open up with all guns, their fire directed out to sea. I do not know the reason for this, but I suppose it was to further subdue the beaten remnants of Rommel's army aboard our ships.

By the time the prisoners had disembarked into barges and been taken to a prisoner of war camp, more empty ships had arrived, to form quite a large convoy for the run back to Gibraltar. Once there, some ships turned north for the U.K., but we, with about twenty others, headed west towards New York. During the crossing, we ran into a very severe gale, in which the convoy had to heave to, because some of the American Liberty ships developed cracks in their welded plates. Luckily, the gale abated before any broke their backs. Later, all the welded American Liberty ships had to have a band of steel plates studded with rivets, to strengthen them.

We went to Bridgeport, Connecticut, to load a similar cargo to previous ones, and as soon as there were enough ships to make up a convoy we set sail again. This time we had a good crossing on our return to Italy. Once more, in Gibraltar, we met more ships from the U.K. In this convoy, we were stationed third ship in the left hand column, with the main part of the convoy on our starboard side. Having already made one run through the Mediterranean without being attacked, we were feeling reasonably safe.

One evening, just before sunset and with the sea very calm, the bosun and I were playing chess on deck, right aft, just about over the ship's propeller. It was the bosun's move and I was just looking around when,

Chess with the Captain

suddenly, I spotted some aircraft, quite high up, off our port quarter. I said to the bosun," We've got a good escort tonight, Bose." Then I saw tracer shells, as though our fighters were in amongst them, although those tracer shells might just as well have been a signal for them to attack. "Christ, Bose," I said, "they're enemy planes."

Up went the chess board. "Action Stations," shouted the bosun. I called through a port hole into the mess-room, "Action Stations. Enemy Attack!"

"Pull the other one," somebody shouted.

I ran along the port side towards the Oerlikon gun on the port side of the bridge. I was just about level with our funnel when I saw one plane diving straight for us. I suppose, on reflection, that it was probably a Stuka dive-bomber. I could not hear it, but it grew larger and larger, in a matter of seconds. Not knowing whether to run forward, run back, or duck, I ducked. The ship shuddered. There was no large bang, but about twelve feet ahead of me was a large, gaping hole in the deck. I could not go forward now, so I ran back aft, just in time to collect all the debris raining down. By this time, the whole convoy had opened up with all their guns; some were aiming very low, for I could hear cannon shells whizzing by.

I was lucky to get away with nothing worse than a cut on my upper left arm. There was a lot of blood, but when this was cleaned off there was nothing much to show. Our funnel and life-boats had gone. Apparently, the plane had hit our funnel on his way up. The engineers and engineering crew on duty at the time had all been killed, and the engine room was on fire. In a matter of minutes the attack was over. Three ships had been hit, all on the outside column: the ship astern of us and the ship behind her, as well as ourselves.

We had no pumps to fight the fire with, and were pulling up buckets of water from over the side, which was absolutely useless. The ship's engine room was a raging inferno and the fuel was alight. One of the escorting corvettes pulled alongside, to within hailing distance, and said he would come back shortly and let us use his pumps. He did not come back. One of the ships behind us must have been in more urgent need of help than us. Eventually, the captain gave the order to abandon ship and we slid the life-rafts over the side. All the ship's life-boats had been destroyed.

The bosun ordered me to take charge of the forward port raft and about eight Asians from the engine room crew, most of whom could not speak English. They were lowering down suitcases and parcels, but there was no room for luggage on the raft, and most of their belongings had to be dumped over the side. There were paddles on the rafts, but it was difficult to get them to paddle in the right direction, and we were just turning round and round. However, being nearly alongside a ship that was burning fiercely and carrying a cargo of explosives did not seem to be a very healthy predicament to be in. I eventually got them all paddling in the right direction, and we pulled away from her. It was dark by now, and an hour or so later a corvette picked us out with a searchlight, and took us aboard.

Chess with the Captain

This corvette also picked up two German airmen, probably the ones who had hit us, one of whom was quite badly injured. The ship was still burning fiercely as the corvette got under way. We were taken to a survivors' camp in Algiers. I and other members of the crew were to be there for about three weeks, and hundreds of others had been there for much longer than that, waiting for transport home. It was a terrible place to be in. Before eating food, we had to pick the flies off our plates. If you were not prepared to do that, you went without. Although we could go into Algiers, we had no money with which to buy food in the town.

After we had been there for three weeks, or so, we heard a rumour that a ship had arrived to take some of us home. It was the Cunard ship *Franconia*, which had been fitted out as a troopship. There were tiers of bunks, three and four high, in the ship's hold. We came home in convoy, the ship packed with survivors, including some women, A.T.S., nurses and others. Being as my allotted bunk was below the water-line, the sound of depth charges exploding sounded very ominous. Next day, word went round that a U-boat had been destroyed.

I had quite a few games of chess with different people. There were lots of card schools being played, pontoon, brag et cetera, with cards that had seen better days. Ossie had nowhere to stay in the U.K., so I asked him if he would like to come home and stay with me. He agreed, and so, at Liverpool, we boarded a train and headed for London. We had three weeks survivors' leave due, but Ossie said that he would try and get a ship that was going to Australia, as soon as possible.

Working on Borth's sea defences in the 1950's

Invitation to the Dance

Ossie stayed with me at my mother's house for about a week, often visiting the shipping office in search of a ship to take him home. During his stay, he asked me if I knew of any dances in the neighbourhood, as he fancied a night out. I took him to the only place that I knew of where there might be dancing, the Welcome Inn at Well Hall Road, Eltham, Kent, and when we arrived, it seemed as if there was a dance being held there nearly every night.

I could not dance, so I stayed in the bar while Ossie went onto the dance floor. Later in the evening, he came back into the bar and introduced me to the girl he had been dancing with. We were to go to the Welcome Inn nearly every night after that. I got to know the girl, Violet, very well, and it turned out that we were to marry about twelve months later. After Ossie left for Australia, I continued to visit the Welcome Inn nearly every night, and Violet often tried to get me onto the dance floor, but I was hopeless. However, we got on very well, and I used to meet her when she finished work at Woolwich.

When my leave was up, I reported to the shipping office, where I discovered that the only ship which required an A/B was an old coaster called *Sulev*, a Estonian ship. I joined her at Tilbury Docks, where she was loading small arms and ammunition. We sailed on the tide, and I soon found that most of the Estonian crew could not speak English. In a convoy of about sixteen ships, we set out to cross the Channel, apparently headed for Ghent, Belgium. The crossing was made at night, but the convoy was attacked by E-boats, and two ships were hit; one of them, which blew up with a blinding flash, could have been a small tanker.

As we sailed up river to Ghent, we could see, from our port side, the vapour trails of V2 rockets being launched. Once we had been unloaded, we set off back to Tilbury, to re-load a cargo of small arms ammunition, a daylight crossing this time, with no losses. I cannot remember where we went after that, but I can remember sailing down the Irish Sea on a very calm day. I was on the wheel, when the captain suddenly grabbed hold of my arm and led me over to the starboard side of the bridge. He pointed down at the ship's wake, and in his broken English he exclaimed how straight it was, which I thought was odd!

The Estonian bosun fell sick, and the captain asked me if I would like to take over his job, and I agreed. Not long afterwards, I realised that it was useless me being in charge of a crew that could not understand English, so I left the ship. The advantage of having been on a coaster was the opportunities it gave for getting home more often, and now I was courting, I did not want to find myself on a ship that might be heading to Australia, so now I joined one of the London Power Company's ships trading between

Chess with the Captain 51

Battersea Power Station and Cardiff, or Swansea. I cannot recall the name of her, although I might remember it again if I saw the names of the company ships in use at the time, in 1944. All these ships were named after the old London boroughs.

I was a bit apprehensive at the prospect of steering the ship under the many Thames bridges to Battersea, and I was hoping that the river pilot might have his own helmsman, but no, the A/Bs were expected to take over their watch. The short mast was lowered as we approached Tower Bridge, and although Tower Bridge would be opened for us, the funnel had to be lowered and replaced at each of the other bridges. Approaching London Bridge, I can remember the pilot giving me aiming points, such as a church spire, by which to steer, and as we passed under each arch he would keep saying, "Good, good. Keep her there. Good." There did not seem to be much space to spare, for we were a fair sized vessel; I suppose she was 250 feet long, and of about 3,000 tons. I cannot remember ever taking a ship down river, light, at least, not under the bridges.

On these ships we had to cook our own food, which was something different, and the watches, of course, were four hours on and four hours off, but the trips were only short ones, round the coast, keeping to the swept channels. I stayed with that company until just before I got married.

During this period, Doodle-Bugs, or Flying Bombs, were coming over London with monotonous regularity, and on the evening before our wedding, we were taking two suitcases full of glassware to Violet's home in Eltham, Kent, and were just going past the Garrison Church at Woolwich, on a tram, when a doodle-bug stopped right overhead. It was a direct hit on the Garrison Church, the tram driver was killed, and everyone on the tram, including me, dived for cover. All the glass in the tram was blown out, I sustained a cut over my left eye, and many people were slightly injured. So we had to carry the two suitcases the last three miles to Eltham.

While our wedding ceremony was taking place on the following day, another flying bomb stopped right over the church, and we all had to dive for cover, including the vicar. The bomb landed about 500 yards away.

The next time I reported to the shipping office, there were no ships available, and I was told to report back next week. My father-in-law was a foreman carpenter for a firm, under contract to the Ministry of Works, busy repairing and making safe bomb-damaged buildings, and he suggested finding me employment with them on what he said was essential work, so I went to work with them.

After the war, I started as a crane driver, with a company called Tuff & Hoar, at a wharf on the Thames, at Woolwich, South East London, where I stayed for a few years. After that I drove cranes on civil engineering sites, on various contracts. In 1055, I was sent to the small Welsh holiday village of Borth, in Cardiganshire, about seven miles north of Aberystwyth. The contract was to drive the Australian redwood piles to form groynes on the beach, and to build a sea wall with a walkway on its top.

I drove the machine to drive the piles, and was helped by a gang of local men, some of whom, to this day, 5th April, 1992, I still meet occasionally at Aberystwyth; sadly, quite a few have since died. On the other side of the road from where I was working was a house to let. After telephoning the owner, I was offered it on a five-year lease. As my wife and I had two sons and no permanent home at this time, we took the lease and moved in. It was a detached house, named 'Surrey', and it had eight bedrooms, and plenty of space to take summer visitors. I had often had to find temporary accommodation for my family at different contract sites, but this time, when the contract was completed, we had all come to like Borth, and we decided to stay on, so I had to find a local job.

At about this time, in 1957, I saw an advertisement which had been placed by the B.B.C. in the Cambrian News, the local newspaper, asking for a rigger for the television mast at Blaen Plwyf, about six or seven miles south of Aberystwyth. It was to be a full-time, superannuated job; I applied and got the position, subject to a medical, when they could arrange it.

My duty was to go up the 500 feet tall mast and inspect the cable couplings, replace any light bulbs that had failed and generally see to anything that required attention. I had been working there for two or three weeks, going up and down the mast, when the station director told me that my medical had been arranged. After an X-ray revealed that I had a spot on my lung, I was sent to Machynlleth Chest Hospital, where I spent the next three months. Full marks go to the doctors and nurses who treated me. I was also lucky in finding a fellow patient who was a chess player. He worked for the Cambrian News, and we were both of about the same playing ability, and spent many hours playing chess. When I was discharged from hospital, I was advised not to start work again for about twelve months. With my sick pay, and income from the visitors or students staying at 'Surrey', we managed to cope financially.

When the twelve months were almost up, I asked my doctor if it was alright for me to return to work, and he agreed that it was, so I started painting and decorating. After I had done one small job for a neighbour, word got around and the work started to come in. I signed off the sick list and was soon earning enough to make ends meet.

During the summer months, quite a few visitors used to come to the side door of 'Surrey' and ask for water, or even to boil water et cetera, so much so that I thought it might be a good place for a café, for Borth has an 18-hole golf course and quite a nice beach.

Out of the blue, the house was offered to us to buy, as sitting tenants, but as a recently self-employed person, I could not raise a mortgage, as I did not have balance sheets going back at least three years. It so happened that I landed quite a large contract to paint and paper a whole property located quite near to 'Surrey', which had just been purchased by a retired,

Welsh-speaking farmer. In casual conversation I mentioned to him that 'Surrey' was for sale and I could not raise the mortgage. When I told him the asking price, he said, "I'll buy it, and keep you on as tenants."

"In that case, Mr. Jones," I said, "would you be prepared to advance me a mortgage instead?"

He agreed, so I bought 'Surrey', and at a reasonable rate of interest. A few months later I had plans drawn up for a café to be built on the southern side of the property. It was very successful, and I paid off the mortgage within three years. My wife and I ran that café for 25 years, until I retired at 65. It gave us a good living all year round, although the trade was only seasonal, from about March to October, and we worked long hours, seven days a week.

Looking back after living in Borth for 35 years, I regret not having learnt to speak Welsh, for most of my chess and golfing friends and my neighbours were Welsh-speakers. My only excuse is that they all, also, spoke English, probably better than I do. Even today, in 1992, I still occasionally meet, in Aberystwyth, the Mr. Jones who was kind enough to advance me that mortgage.

I have no regrets for my 35 years in Borth; I cannot claim to be Welsh, but I find myself supporting the Welsh in all sporting events et cetera.

I make no claims of my ability to play chess; I just consider myself to be an average player, who enjoys a game, win or lose. I look on my life as one big chess game. I have made quite a lot of bad moves, and some good ones. This book is probably my last move.

Will it be a lost game? Stale mate, or check-mate!

It was reading *Shaw, Savill & Albion, The Post-war Fortunes of a Shipping Empire* by Richard P. De Kerbrech, that brought to mind the memories of my voyages on the *Waimarama*, and the consequences, which I can assure my readers are all quite true.

Obviously, I am not proud of deserting *Waimarama* and the Australian Army - far from it. But I feel that I did my best during World War II, and my excuse for the train of events I have just related is that it all came about through PLAYING CHESS WITH THE CAPTAIN.

Footnote:

I am aware, of course, that with the present day means of communications, fax machines, et cetera, someone somewhere, with access to such equipment, might get the urge to check some of the facts of this story. For instance, I would think that Australian Army records in Sydney would probably confirm that I joined up in Sydney, in 1941, as Harold Austin Samson. (If so, I would like very much to know if I got my army number correct?)

Also, the shipping office at Townsville might have records to prove that a Cyril Thompson signed on a ship named the *Fort Pine*, which was being loaded with sugar by an army unit called a Dock Operating Unit, or Regiment, some time in 1941/1942, under instruction of dockers, and if there is anyone who might have been on *Fort Pine* at that time, I might even be able to prove that Cyril Thompson took her out of Townsville Harbour, under the orders of the pilot, of course.